Striving
While Black!

A Playbook for the Seriously Ambitious

Getting to Your Goal–Without Losing Your Soul!

By Kwame S. Salter

TALENT TRUMPS!™
Change is Inevitable - Growth Is Optional

CONTENTS

The chapters in this book are short but rich in content. Each chapter represents a distillation of over 30 years of management experience and executive leadership. The following summaries give you an idea of the focus of each chapter.

FOREWARD

Most people have a skill set; Kwame Salter has that plus a gift set. At various stages of his career, Kwame's gifts have empowered him to be a highly successful businessman, elected public official, civil rights activist, and educator. As a scholar and practitioner, he has "been there, done that!"

The gifts of insight, discernment and elucidation are central to Kwame's

(handwritten annotations: (JUDGE *ABILITY* WELL) above "discernment"; (MAKE *TO* CLEAR) above "elucidation")

gift set. He sees what others do not; he puts the "evil eye" on what is in view; and he is able to explain his observations in ways that enable others to share in his understandings. He is able quickly to "defuzz" issues and concepts to prove that the complex is often merely complicated—and unnecessarily so.

Striving While Black is Exhibit A of Kwame's gifts. Without fluff and folderol, this slim text gives Black aspirants—and any upwardly mobile professional in any field—the coaching required to arrive at higher stages with both soul and integrity intact. *Striving While Black* is portable, readable, witty, exceptional, and highly recommended. Buy, read, learn.

John Y. Odom, Ph.D.

SECTION ONE: GET READY

Chapter 1: DO YOUR HOMEWORK
Prepare and gather intelligence even before you approach the targeted company.

Chapter 2: AVOID STEREOTYPICAL BEHAVIORS
Sidestep the mistaken notion that you need to show white people you are different from them and really "down" with black culture.

SECTION TWO: GET SET

Chapter 3: INTEGRATE THE LUNCHES AND LINKS
Avoid isolating yourself from non-work activities.

Chapter 4: MASTER THE JOB
Insure the most fundamental aspect of career success.

SECTION THREE: GO FOR IT

Chapter 5: MANAGE PERCEPTION
Influence how people view and interpret your actions and behavior.

Chapter 6: BE A DEPENDABLE SUPPLIER
Examine how the internal work environment is made up of both suppliers and customers.

Chapter 7: BUILD AND NURTURE A SUPPORT NETWORK
Establish for yourself the importance of a network of mentors and advocates.

DEDICATION

This first book is dedicated with undying love, respect and admiration to my father, Samuel L. Salter, Sr. My father was my role model, teacher and, to me and my siblings, "My Daddy." "My Daddy" taught me how to be a man. More importantly, he taught me how to carry myself with dignity, strength and a sense of purpose as a black man in America. I will never forget his warning to me as I entered the world as an adult black male. He simply stated, "Son, white America tends to view blacks in one of only two ways—as superhuman or subhuman. You have got to work harder and show that you are better. You can't be average. You have got to be better than the best." To S. L. Salter, the father, the professional educator for over 40 years, the proud black man and activist, I dedicate this book.

ACKNOWLEDGEMENTS

First, heartfelt appreciation to my wife, Phyllis V. Harris, who by virtue of our relationship was a captive sounding board helping me sort through what I was experiencing during my corporate career.

To my late father and mother, Samuel and Reva Salter, who dared me to be the best I could be and then provided the love, prodding, support and wisdom to achieve my goals.

To my children Kevin, Keri, Matt and Lauren, who shared with me their experiences as young, gifted and black talents. Their questions and insights helped me stay current, and their coachability allowed me to test out some of the theories discussed in this book.

To my late brother, George, and my very alive sister, Grace, who always encouraged me to go after all my dreams and never hesitated to show their pride in me and my accomplishments. Never was there sibling rivalry—always sibling support.

Special thanks go to Dr. John Y. Odom, a brilliant and provocative thinker. Over the years, Dr. Odom has provided me with insights, perspectives and support as I navigated my way through the whitewater rapids of corporate America. It was Dr. Odom who encouraged me to start writing down my observations.

To Terry M. Faulk, retired Executive Vice President, Human Resources at Kraft, who as a wonderful mentor, friend and boss, never allowed race, color or gender to get in the way of identifying, developing and deploying the best people. This former Marine could best be described as hard but fair, with emphasis on fair.

Finally, to Jerry Heigel, retired Chairman and CEO of Oscar Mayer Foods, who was relentless in recruiting me to work for him. If ever there were a person who shot straight and was always in a mano-a-mano posture, it was Jerry. He told me what to expect as a black man in corporate America and how he would support and empower me to change the white male culture of Oscar Mayer.

FOR MY PEOPLE
By Margaret Walker

For my people everywhere singing their slave songs
repeatedly: their dirges and their ditties and their blues
and jubilees, praying their prayers nightly to an
unknown god, bending their knees humbly to an
unseen power;

For my people lending their strength to the years, to the
gone years and the now years and the maybe years,
washing ironing cooking scrubbing sewing mending
hoeing plowing digging planting pruning patching
dragging along never gaining never reaping never
knowing and never understanding;

For my playmates in the clay and dust and sand of Alabama
backyards playing baptizing and preaching and doctor
and jail and soldier and school and mama and cooking
and playhouse and concert and store and hair and
Miss Choomby and company;

For the cramped bewildered years we went to school to learn
to know the reasons why and the answers to and the
people who and the places where and the days when, in
memory of the bitter hours when we discovered we
were black and poor and small and different and nobody
cared and nobody wondered and nobody understood;

For the boys and girls who grew in spite of these things to

be man and woman, to laugh and dance and sing and
play and drink their wine and religion and success, to
marry their playmates and bear children and then die
of consumption and anemia and lynching;

For my people thronging 47th Street in Chicago and Lenox
Avenue in New York and Rampart Street in New
Orleans, lost disinherited dispossessed and happy
people filling the cabarets and taverns and other
people's pockets and needing bread and shoes and milk and
land and money and something—something all our own;

For my people walking blindly spreading joy, losing time
being lazy, sleeping when hungry, shouting when
burdened, drinking when hopeless, tied, and shackled
and tangled among ourselves by the unseen creatures
who tower over us omnisciently and laugh;

For my people blundering and groping and floundering in
the dark of churches and schools and clubs
and societies, associations and councils and committees and
conventions, distressed and disturbed and deceived and
devoured by money-hungry glory-craving leeches,
preyed on by facile force of state and fad and novelty, by
false prophet and holy believer;

For my people standing staring trying to fashion a better way
from confusion, from hypocrisy and misunderstanding,
trying to fashion a world that will hold all the people,
all the faces, all the adams and eves and their countless generations;

Let a new earth rise. Let another world be born. Let a bloody peace be written in the sky. Let a second generation full of courage issue forth; let a people loving freedom come to growth. Let a beauty full of healing and a strength of final clenching be the pulsing in our spirits and our blood. Let the martial songs be written, let the dirges disappear. Let a race of men now rise and take control.

(1937)

PROLOGUE

Career Intelligence Quotient (CIQ)

Welcome to the world of work. Or better yet, how's that career goal or dream looking to you right now? Is your trajectory still properly calibrated to take you to your destination position? Careers are funny things. Often what you had planned to accomplish in your career quickly becomes elusive and you slowly become cynical. You did all the right things—went to college, even graduate school, and worked hard at your job. Still, you feel your career has stagnated. No one told you this would happen. The principle of uninterrupted career verticality seems to be a myth. In fact, careers are more like a Stairmaster exercise machine than an escalator. The question now is: How does one effectively negotiate or avoid the often treacherous straits and narrows of corporate politics and the even more insidious barrier of racial stereotyping?

Just how does one scale the mountain of corporate success without some help—like finding some sort of organizational Sherpa guide, a mentor, to point out how you should equip yourself for the journey? Initially, we all think that hard work, discipline and intellect will take us to the top of our professions. Then comes the rude awakening. We apparently lack something. But what exactly do we lack? Is it desire, determination, drive—or, God forbid, is it the smarts we lack?

What is missing is the level of your Career Intelligence Quotient [CIQ], a combination of organizational savvy, interpersonal skills and learning agility. Collectively, position knowledge, skills and ability are the givens that represent the price of admission to your career journey.

Most successful chart climbers have figured out this part of the equation. In other words, you have to have more going for you than just job mastery. You have to be smarter in ways that set you apart from the other worker bees and functional drones that crave face time and good merit increases. You have to use your CIQ to leverage organizational opportunities. To advance, you need to win the first leg of the career Trifecta—**organizational savvy.** For me, organizational savvy is the ability to tease out the norms of any organization before you inadvertently step on one.

Organizational rules and regulations are written, published and distributed for public consumption. Norms, on the other hand, are the organization's invisible land mines. They are never published; they are to be divined. They are more powerful than rules, regulations and policies. Norms not only tell what you cannot do—more importantly, they tell you what is acceptable and what you can and should do.

Pronouncements of rules are for those corporate denizens who need policy to be explicit, unequivocal and consistent. A savvy person apprehends the subtle cues evident to real students of organizational behavior. The quicker you can spot, decipher and internalize the cues, the higher your CIQ.

A lot of these cues have to do with how individuals in the organization treat each other. **Mastering interpersonal skills** is the second leg of the career Trifecta. Interpersonal relationship skills are important in building a fungible type of equity. I call this relationship equity. While it is not transferable outside the organization, it is a highly valuable internal commodity that is useful in moving your career forward.

Real work and accomplishment take place in the white space between jobs. The individual who functions well in this space between your job and a fellow employee's job knows the exact moment when you are the supplier or the customer. Each status provides you with career building opportunities. When you are an internal supplier, people are able to observe your promptness, accuracy and willingness to help them meet a deadline or goal.

When you are a customer, your suppliers are able to determine what type of person you really are—that is, are you clear in your expectations, do you look to place blame, are you reasonable, and would you be someone they could work for as a subordinate? At some point, these fellow employees, either with their words or their silence, will accelerate your career or derail it.

Finally, successful career management depends on how mentally nimble you are in real time situations. **Learning agility,** the final leg of the career trifecta, means you must quickly master shifts in business concepts, organizational constructs and political alliances. The ability to provide either constructive feedback or insightful input to leadership in times of transition will increase your worth and value in the organization. Superficial mastery of these shifts will often get you in trouble. It is equally important to have good questions as to have good answers. When you win on this one and the two aforementioned, it will be obvious to all that you operate with a high CIQ. *Organizational savvy, interpersonal skills, Learning agility*

Striving while black in corporate America means that we will be exposed to new rules, that we must use tools and employ new strategies in managing our careers. Again, the purpose of this book is to help improve your CIQ as a black person in corporate America.

> *You can tell whether a man is clever by his answers...*
> *You can tell whether a man is wise by his questions.*
> *--Naquib Mahfouz*

INTRODUCTION

THE GAME

If you must play, decide upon
three things at the start: the
rules of the game, the stakes,
and the quitting time.
—*Chinese Proverb*

This book was born out of close to 25 years of working, nay striving, in corporate America as an observant black man. Having seen how blacks were and are viewed by this uniquely white culture, I felt it important to share my experiences.

Although this work may not answer all your questions, I believe it is important to share my observations. I am sure many who read this book have reached similar conclusions from their experiences, and I am positive that many others have had markedly different experiences. In either case, blacks too often are confounded and confused by the role race plays in their careers. We often ask ourselves: Is my color the reason I'm getting or not getting needed feedback? Is there a limit on my career trajectory because of my color? Is racism so inculcated in the organizational culture that it trumps talent? These are questions that I routinely bandied about with family, close friends, and associates.

Corporate America is a paradox. The interesting thing that I've observed is that without "black" people there are no "white" people. Before we blacks enter the room, the whites are ethnics—Germans, Irish, Jews, Poles, Italians. The instant a black person enters the room, the ethnics transform into White People. Therefore, I have concluded that white people are a socio-political grouping and not an ethnic classification. Being white has no anthropological or cultural meaning among and between white people—until a black person enters the space. Being white, then, is a power play that allows even the most liberal white to feel a sense of superiority. At the same time, however, blacks have the power to turn ethnics into White People.

In terms of social justice, enlightened business leaders always seem to say and, in many cases, do the right thing. Still, upon closer examination, an element of "do as we say and not as we do" undermines their progressive message. In spite of these messages, young and talented African-Americans in particular—as well as Asians working in non-technology positions and dark-skinned Hispanics—often find that their career trajectories are flat or non-existent. The occasional and newsworthy exceptional minority gracing the business sections of newspapers or national periodicals is not the rule. Could it be that smarts, hard work and loyalty to the company, while necessary, are not sufficient criteria for upward mobility in corporate America?

African-Americans wonder aloud if it's their color that impedes them— or if it is actually an issue of competence. Could it be that their color eclipses their competence in the eyes of many decision makers? Is there something they are missing? Does their cultural heritage hinder them? Are white people so inculcated with racial stereotypes that no matter what they do, they will not measure up? Is it possible that they never got the "playbook" and don't know how to play the game? Are some expecting special consideration because of their background, culture and color? Or is it all of the above? After close to a quarter of a century negotiating power in the corporate world, I am willing to venture an answer. I think it is all of the above.

Success in the corporate environment is elusive, regardless of your color. However, contrary to what the "color blind" adherents claim, both color and culture can become helping or hindering factors in moving up the success ladder. In fact, a hierarchy of color is deeply ingrained in the American psyche—or at least in the African-American psyche. This relative ranking of race is summed up in one those urban short poems we use to quote to explain our lack of mobility in American society—"If you're white, you're all right; if you're yellow, you're a mellow fellow; if you're brown, you can stick around; but if you're black—stay back!"

My purpose in writing this book is simple. I want to share what I learned about how to succeed as a black person in corporate America. I want to share the lessons gleaned from my own and others' experiences while climbing the corporate ladder. I will use an anecdotal style to capture my reflections and offer my insights. Chapters are organized around how to prepare for your first corporate encounter, what to expect once you are in the corporate environment, and how to survive and advance on a playing field that is not always level. What I learned during my journey is applicable to a number of different ethnic groups and, to some extent, everybody. Simply put, my key learnings from my corporate experiences were to master the following five P's.

- **Poise** is the ability to be at ease and comfortable in any situation. As a friend of mine always said, "If you don't know what to say, know what to do—and if you don't know what to do, know what to say." Seek to be "comfortable in your own skin." Too often, we commit blunders and faux pas because we are uncomfortable. We exude a palpable anxiety. We look like we don't belong—ergo, we don't!

- **Presence** is that unique ability to have an impact without sound effects or grand gestures. Presence does not belong to the beautiful, the handsome or the tall. In this case, size really does not matter. Presence is an intangible quality that enraptures and enchants without effort. It is being mysterious without trying; being transparent without artifice; and being gracious and courteous with all. Presence generates an electric quality. Presence causes people to observe you as you enter or leave a room. One source of presence is our color. Before we open our mouths, we are judged. People pay attention to our gestures and expressions. This can be quite advantageous if we are prepared and proud. In a sense, Presence is style, and at every point in your career—corporate aspirants—style matters.

- **Projection** is clarity of speech and communication. For many whites, the highest compliment that can be paid to a black person is that he or she is "articulate." So often, the black person feels insulted, minimized or confused by the compliment. In our mind, we wonder was the compliment more of a statement of surprise—"I didn't expect you to speak so clearly." Probably even more concerning is that rarely does the one complimenting us see the connection between our thought processes and our eloquent words. In their minds, our ability to speak in an articulate manner is not necessarily a sign of our intellectual prowess. Yet to be successful in corporate America, we must be able to say what we mean, mean what we say and all too often even defend what we say.

- **Persistence** is the cornerstone of all successful careers. Yet this often quoted advice sums it up: "Nothing in the world can take the place of persistence. Talent will not; nothing is more common than unsuccessful men with talent. Genius will not; unrewarded genius is almost a proverb. Education will not; the world is full of educated derelicts. Persistence and determination alone are omnipotent. The slogan 'Press On' has solved and always will solve the problems of the human race."

Finally, **Politics** is the allocation of the power, values and resources inherent in the organization. Someone or some group decides who gets what and when. You must recognize that all organizations, including families, are political entities. Let me also say that politics is a game—a high-stakes game with identifiable winners and losers. Moreover, either you play the game or the game plays you.

The best way to handle the politics is to appear to be apolitical. In other words, do not overtly align yourself with any group—but do not shy away from politics. Strive to be pragmatic and not dogmatic. Attempt to ferret out the agendas of individuals and cliques; decide if their agendas support and promote your career interests. Avoid gossip and group think. Strive to become a net importer of information, not a net exporter. Listen without comment when there is a discussion about your boss or peers; ask for clarification and insights on how and why someone is considered a "good guy" or "bad egg." Practice strenuous non-judgment in your statements and behavior.

"Before you join the circus, make every effort to get a peek under the tent. You might be surprised that there are more clowns than highfliers"

—*Kwame S. Salter*

1

CHAPTER

DO YOUR HOMEWORK

The Internet has democratized access to information. You can and should research the company in all possible ways. Find out what they make, how long they have been making it, who their customers are, and how much money they make. Before you interview with your first company, you should identify, investigate, and force rank your potential employers. Do not rely solely on word of mouth, on diversity rankings or awards, or even on the smooth salesmanship of the company recruiter. Do your own homework. Use the tools available to get a "peek under the tent."

The tools include scouring the Internet for facts from the company's website, monitoring unofficial employee "wikis" and discussion boards, asking probing questions of company representatives, and getting inside information from current and former employees. The Internet has given real "power to the people." However, information alone is not real power—access to information is. Today, we each have a staff of researchers, private investigators, fact-checkers and experts who can be accessed and put to work with a few keystrokes.

The best way to approach this data-gathering phase is to heed President Reagan's axiom—"Trust but verify." Sometimes, we are impressed by a company's ranking in well-known black-oriented publications. Use extreme caution in putting too much stock in these "diversity awards" because sometimes these are paybacks for advertising heavily in the publication. There is nothing wrong with acknowledging the company's "supplier diversity efforts" so long as you corroborate the information. Just because a company directs a small percentage of its advertising and consumer promotion dollars to minority enterprises doesn't mean it is a good place for so-called "minorities" to work.

Perhaps the most controversial databases for you to mine are the unofficial employee forums that serve as wikis for disenchanted or angry employees, either current or former. These sources are worth looking into as long as you keep in mind that the tone is skewed towards those employees who are dissatisfied or have an unresolved beef. Do not dismiss this portal. Consider all the information you receive as data points to use in your decision making process.

The most accurate and useful data comes from active employees. They can tell you how the family portrait differs from the reality. Ask questions like:

- What's the day-to-day work environment really like?
- In what functions are most blacks congregated?
- Who are the most senior blacks and what are their titles?
- What was the biggest disconnect you've experienced between the recruiter's words and your actual experience once on board?
- Are the middle management supervisors fair and objective?
- Are opportunities for development and growth readily available?
- What routes are blacks given in the sales function—predominantly inner city or low margin routes?
- Is an affirmative action rationale used when hiring or promoting blacks? Are blacks represented in the talent pipeline, and how long have they been idling there?

In summary, use the Internet, recruiters and active employees as a way of getting underneath the canned message employers use to lure potential employees. Find out three features of the company's record:

1) Is the company viable? What is their record of reductions-in-force (RIFs) and when was the last RIF?

2) Is the company inclusive in attracting, developing and retaining people of color, as well as showcasing them in marketing and advertising?

3) Are prospective employees of color recruited by Human Resources (HR) or the hiring manager—or both?

In other words, who wants you most, the HR function or the business? And for what reasons—to improve the "optics" of the company's profile or to bring you in to add value to the company's mission?

People join a company and quit a boss.

The role and script for the "glad to be here" Negro were written by whites—yet no one has ever played the role more convincingly than the insecure black man.

—Kwame S. Salter

2

CHAPTER

AVOID STEREOTYPICAL BEHAVIORS

Your color makes it difficult or unnecessary for many whites to view you as a unique individual beyond racial dimensions. In their minds, the range of variability for you is limited based on the steady diet of stereotypes that the media feeds them about the types of blacks they will encounter. The lesson in this chapter is to open up to who you really are socially and culturally. For every stereotype, real persons embody those stereotypical traits and behaviors. Yes, there are blacks who live the thug life; who play the minstrel for whites; who are exceptional—but often not articulate—athletes and entertainers. But as A.G. Gaston, the pioneering black insurance company millionaire from Alabama, once said, "I would rather be able to say that I is rich than I am poor."

In much greater numbers are blacks who contradict the stereotypes. Nevertheless, white America and a sizable percentage of blacks view The Cosby Show as less representative of our lifestyle and culture than the offerings of Tyler Perry. What's the deal? Will the real black person please step forward?

The reality is that black culture is not a monolith. Black culture cannot be bottled and dispensed in the timeframes of a sitcom. However, white America has found it much easier to view all of black culture through a single lens. And many black Americans find it easier to accept these distortions than to challenge them. Ironically, the very ones who are uncomfortable around their own in black social settings tend to mimic these so-called "ghetto" blacks when around their white counterparts. Often, inner-city slang and behaviors are displayed as a cultural badge of honor by upwardly mobile black professionals. The results for these "buppies" is a weird and existential sense of alienation from both blacks and whites.

Because of this alienation, there is a need to connect, to be part of some group. And even if we are acculturated as whites, our hue dictates that we should behave as black. Consequently, we slip into the role of expert commentator inside and outside the company on all matters involving blacks and on questions like "Are all black people supporting Obama?" "Do all blacks believe OJ is innocent?" and "How do your people want to be referred to—blacks, African-Americans, Negroes or colored?" Some argue that this type of inquiry is good for promoting dialogue between the races. I submit that it is a less a dialogue and more a monologue that would be offensive if the tables were turned.

Our black culture is rich with nuance, wisdom and uniqueness. Part of what we bring to corporate America is a perspective that is not transparent to marketing mavens in the boardroom. Instead of reinforcing media stereotypes, why not exploit and market the richness and uniqueness of our culture? For example, Kraft Foods found out how blacks altered its iconic Mac & Cheese, adopted its Sandwich Spread as a key ingredient in killer potato salads, and put fruit in the ever popular Kool Aid. As a result, Kraft used these insights to improve their sales among blacks and other ethnic minority groups. Really knowing your culture can be both a career- and business-building opportunity.

> *We are what we pretend to be, so we must be careful about what we pretend to be.*
> —*Kurt Vonnegut*

Official channels of information are always scooped by the informal chatter on the social grapevine—be there or be square.

—*Kwame S. Salter*

3
CHAPTER

INTEGRATE THE LUNCHES AND THE LINKS

The fact of the matter is that any gathering of employees—on or off the clock—is an opportunity to learn something that could be advantageous to you in performing your job and managing your career. Go to a bar after work and listen to some country western, hard rock or popular music you might not have on your iPod.

How many times have you heard or said, "I have been around these white folks all day and week. I am not going to spend my free time with them"? Sounds like you need a cultural respite—a timeout from acting white. Not so fast, my friends. Sometimes a few hours invested in cross-cultural events and activities will yield quite a bounty of information. Remember the adage, "He who controls the flow of information, controls the situation."

Official communications about company direction, strategy and decisions are usually "a day late and a dollar short." The grapevine is still the best way to intercept official communiqués, to get out in front of news—good and bad. Where is the confidential information most often traded? In formal planning meetings?—Nope. In official company memos and press releases?—Nope. In staff meetings?—Again, nope.

The reality is that highly confidential information is most freely traded in social gatherings—lunches, golf outings, after-work get-togethers, and bowling, softball, volleyball or basketball leagues. If you want to get the heads up, you must show up. What's wrong with spending time after work with some colleagues over a beer or two? It doesn't matter if you're not a scratch golfer—just be a good listener.

One very important caveat is not to repeat to anyone what you have heard. Listening is the key. Too much talking works against you. Keep the information to yourself, for yourself and for your advantage. Avoid the temptation to be first with the scoop. As the Tao Te Ching states, "Those who know don't talk, and those that talk don't know." Strive to be a net importer, not exporter, of information.

Another reason social integration is so important in corporate America is because our white colleagues and bosses know very little about us—how we grew up, what we are like as individuals, and what aspirations and values define us. All of these unknowns about us impact the way we are viewed as employees. Often the boss is hesitant to give us constructive feedback for fear of being labeled a racist. A supervisor's problem is having no context for interpreting our responses.

In the minds of many whites, we were hired to meet a diversity or affirmative action goal. Reduced to being a statistic—a highly combustible one that the supervisor has to manage—we lack dimension as a whole person. This imposed status as a mere corporate diversity recruit rather than as a value-added talent creates an artificial but real barrier to our being considered a full member of the lodge. It is easy to be detached or even hostile to someone you consider alien or, at best, tangential. We must resist the impulse to act the same way toward the organization as it does toward us. The reality is that practicing black separatism in corporate America doesn't help you. We must continue to be present; to sit-in; to integrate not only the buildings and grounds but, more importantly, the corporate culture.

If you are setting out to merely be the best Negro teacher, the best Negro doctor, the best Negro lawyer...you have already flunked your matriculation exam into the University of Integration.

--Dr. Martin Luther King, Jr.

Talk is cheap and excuses are lame.
Competency speaks volumes
                              —Kwame S. Salter

4

CHAPTER

MASTER THE JOB

Competency is the quality of being adequately prepared physically and mentally for a particular undertaking. Knowing what to do and being proficient in the nuts and bolts of a job (technical competence) is one thing; how you do your job in relationship to other employees and your boss (behavioral competence) is quite another thing. Too many blacks approach these two competencies as though they are independent variables, but these two competencies work hand in hand. People skills go with technical skills; being a competent master of a task is no protection against a job action for being a jerk.

The first order of business is to figure out exactly what is expected of you in your job and determine if you have the requisite knowledge, skills and abilities to do that job. Too

frequently, we accept a job based on what someone thinks
the job is or should be. Instead, you really need to know the
specific tasks, duties and responsibilities that make up the job.
Does what I bring to the job fit what needs to be done? Is there
a written description? Is this description current? No matter
how gifted or talented a new person in a position is, no one
comes into a job fully up to speed. It just will not happen.

There is a definite process for attaining competency, which
involves awareness, understanding and mastery. Several years
ago, I heard this process broken down into four phases:
-     Unconscious Incompetence
-     Conscious Incompetence
-     Unconscious Competence
-     Conscious Competence

We come into a job not knowing what we don't know. This
is Unconscious Incompetence. This is the period of trial and
error and "fake it till you make it." We project a confident
demeanor; we say we know a particular approach is risky
to pretend it's a calculated risk; we put forth points of
view intended to impress though we are actually devoid
of certainty. Our learning curve is steep and fraught with
anxiety.

During this phase, feedback is intense and swift. And it is
during this phase that well-meaning colleagues and good
bosses come to the rescue. They point out in very clear terms
what we need to know to be successful in the position.
With their help, we are on track to the next phase of gaining
competence—Conscious Incompetence. In this new phase, we

are beginning to know what we don't know. At this point, we become conscious of the voids in our knowledge, skills and abilities needed to do the job in an acceptable manner.

Conscious Incompetence is a critical phase in our development because we identify and isolate specific areas of development needed to be successful in this job. It is during this phase that the performance appraisal process becomes more than just perfunctory. To use an athletic term, this is where we start to become "fundamentally sound." We begin to grasp the nuts and bolts of the job—the what and the how of performance. The job requirements begin to make more sense to us. We are even able to help newbies who, like us not too long ago, are trying to get their heads around the what and how of doing their own new jobs.

As we begin to share our knowledge of job requirements with others, a strange thing happens. We become aware of what we are good at. This zone of awareness is moving us toward Conscious Competence. During this phase we exude confidence in our ability to do what is expected. We take initiative without getting approval at each step of the process, we see opportunities for improvement, and we feel the job getting smaller and less daunting. Out of the ashes of our uncertainty, fear of failure and just plain ignorance, we rise like the mythical Phoenix.

As the great boxer Muhammad Ali once said, "I am not cocky. I'm confident." We think we know what we know. However, the next phase moves us back into our unconscious realm— this time to Unconscious Competence. We discover that we hadn't known how much we really do know. Much of how we perform our jobs becomes routine and automatic. This is revealed when we struggle to explain what we do every day and what our job really requires from us. We are in that phase when an objective party observing us can tell us what we do and how we do it.

This is the phase when instincts informed by experience kick in to enhance our performance, when we begin to question how we "pulled it off." This is when we are even becoming a bit bored because we have seen every business cycle, every seasonal surprise and every annual crisis.

If we are not aware of ourselves, we can easily slip into cynicism. We find ourselves not having the time or patience to deal with new employees in their own fledgling phases of competency development. This is when we should be looking to reignite our passion. This might involve an expanded role in our existing job or a rotational assignment to a lower level job. For example, consider becoming a mentor or moving out of your comfort zone by transitioning to a different role.

> *There are no menial jobs, only menial attitudes.*
> *--William John Bennett*

Who you going to believe? Me or your lying eyes?

—Richard Pryor

5

CHAPTER

<u>MANAGE PERCEPTIONS</u>

Often, what we intend to communicate about ourselves and our motives is obscured and misinterpreted because we let others draw conclusions without any input from us. <u>We should always be vigilant about how we are being perceived. Sometimes it is simply best to ask, "How am I doing? What advice can you give me?"</u> This line of questioning allows us to clarify and manage what we intend the person to see or know about us. We have a tendency to think we can dictate how others see us. Over our lifetime, we have practiced certain facial expressions, voice inflections and gestures that we use to project to others how we want them to perceive us.

Sometimes these little visual cues work. We have convinced

people that we are what we really are not, or that we feel what we really do not feel. At best fleeting, these little manipulations are difficult to sustain. As the old adage says, "If you can fake sincerity over an extended period, you've got it made." But how we look or what we say does not matter—what counts is how we act or behave over time.

The Latin word persona, or "mask," was the basis of the famed psychologist Carl Jung's coinage of the term "outward or social personality." We all have developed an exterior social personality for public consumption. In other words, in social settings who we really are might not be who we want people to think we are. Our social personality or mask can be useful, especially if it results in winning friends and influencing people. On the other hand, it can be a devious technique to throw people off the scent of our true, less appealing, core personality. I am recommending that we work to align our social personalities as closely as possible to our daily environments. Managing Perception is a balancing act between who we really are and how people see us in relationship to themselves.

Performance evaluations are perhaps the most vivid example of how perceptions can impact one's career trajectory. Too often, the evaluation process is overly subjective and rife with bias—some good and some bad, depending on how well you sync with your boss. In their seminal textbook, Human Resources Management, authors Robert L. Mathis and John H. Jackson introduce the concept of "rater bias," which includes:

- Varying Standards, when bosses apply different

standards and expectations for employees performing similar jobs;

•	Recency and Primacy Effects, or the "What have you done for me lately?" effect;

•	Rater Bias, when a rater's unconscious or quite unintentional values or prejudices distort the rating and have a negative impact;

•	Halo and Horns Effect, when a rater scores an employee high [halo] on all job criteria because of performance in one area or when a low rating on one characteristic leads to an overall low rating [horns];

•	Contrast Error, which is the tendency to rate people relative to others rather than against performance standards. For example, if everyone else performs at a mediocre level, then a person performing somewhat better may be rated as excellent because of the contrast effect; and

•	Similar-to-Me/Different-from-Me Errors, which for me is the most arbitrary and pernicious because raters are influenced by whether people show characteristics that are the same as or different from their own.

Too often, the characteristics we are judged on are beyond our control—beyond our color and culture. It is this bias that most often negatively affects blacks in the corporate world. Still, we should not expect to be exempt from performance evaluations. Rather, we should prepare ourselves.

The most important step in mental preparation is to put the evaluation event in perspective. In other words, think about the session as a developmental opportunity, not as a definitive event. Viewing the session as developmental allows you to go into the conversation expecting to receive constructive feedback. Any evaluation session that focuses only on your strengths shortchanges you by undermining your ability to become better in your current or future jobs. Even before the formal session and without equivocation, tell the boss that you see yourself as a top performer and are open to being rigorously managed as such—every day. This shows that you are willing to take blunt, critical feedback that is so necessary to getting better in your current position and reaching your career goals.

If you approach the evaluation with trepidation, a mental block caused by emotional tension arises and you forget to mention something you normally can do or have done. You become defensive. Neither a defensive nor an offensive posture is helpful in becoming mentally prepared for the evaluation.

Employing the developmental approach allows you to frame a strategy based on honesty, integrity and truth. You are able to assess honestly the quality of your performance against goals, to possess the integrity to admit the missed opportunities, and to tell the truth about why you did or didn't reach your stated goals. Your going-in strategy is based on disarming the boss—who, most likely, is prepared to argue with you about your accepting your shortcomings.

Once the session begins, listen carefully and take notes; try to isolate the performance deficiency the boss is alluding to or identifying specifically; ask questions only for clarity and deeper understanding—not as challenges to the boss's assessment. Finally, after listening intently without interrupting, rephrase what you heard and ask if you accurately decoded what he/she said. If there is agreement that you heard what was intended, respond only to those points that are unclear to you or are based on incomplete information. If the boss has incomplete information, it is likely that you failed to post him/her when the problem initially arose. Accept responsibility and offer to provide the missing information. If it appears that the boss is inflexible and incorrect, agree to disagree and ask how to remedy the situation. Throughout this session, you must stay on course by demonstrating poise, presence and a clear projection of your willingness to be managed for excellence.

Too often, others in the workplace pre-determine the social personality of persons of color based on their own myths, cultural ignorance or blatant racism. Our challenge is to manage and correct these erroneous perceptions. For example, at work when we display passion or excitement about a particular idea or initiative, we are told right away to "calm down." As a manager giving feedback, we may be accused of being "intimidating." As a colleague, when we ignore slights and insults—both intended and unintended—in an effort to be civil, we may be viewed as "happy-go-lucky." These erroneous perceptions, left uncorrected, reinforce stereotypes that devalue our individuality and allow non-blacks to be oblivious to our desire to excel.

The key to managing perceptions at work starts with being aware of the difference between the cultural milieu we grew up in and the sterile culture of corporate America. In corporate America, being dispassionate, calculating and anal are valued traits—when not taken to the extreme. I am not suggesting that we deny who we are in terms of our culturally influenced behaviors. Instead, we should become keenly aware of what behaviors work and in what situations these behaviors are less subject to distortion and misunderstanding.

We must develop a corporate game face. Specifically, one should be aware of what humor is appropriate in the workplace, what presentation style is standard and valued, and what represents the outer limits—both casual and business—of meeting attire. Never, never, however, give up your individuality and personal style. Just be aware of what you are saying, doing, and wearing. Remember, work is not a Thanksgiving family dinner, nor is it a sports event or a night on the town.

We don't see things as they are, we see them as we are...
--Anais Nin

The real question your fellow employee has for you is, "What have you done for me, lately?" If you can answer that question without "hubba, hubba" or stuttering, you win!

                    --Kwame S. Salter

6
CHAPTER

BE A DEPENDABLE SUPPLIER

Work gets done in the organizational white spaces between jobs. When you need something from a fellow employee to get your job done, you're a customer. When you need to get something to a fellow employee to facilitate his or her getting a task done, you're a supplier. It is easier being a customer than a supplier. Yet a dependable supplier is highly regarded and valued. Being a dependable supplier allows you to build relationship equity. The best way to get your career noticed is to notice someone else's. In the corporate world, noticing someone means helping him/her get their job done. In that sense, you are a crucial supplier.

Once you get the reputation of being a responsive and dependable colleague, you will develop a cadre of supporters who sing your praises—even when you're not in the room. Everybody has a clearly defined or presumed set of task, duties and responsibilities—that is, a job. On an organizational chart, jobs may appear to be discrete, independent and free-floating entities. In reality, jobs are interconnected, interdependent and overlapping entities. No person or job is a self-sufficient island. To get desired results, employees are dependent on timely help from each other. Sometimes, you need inputs (you're the customer) from a fellow employee, and at other times, you need to provide inputs (you're the supplier).

This exchange of inputs takes place in the space between the customer and supplier. This space is often referred to as white space; it is in this white space that workplace reputations are made or broken, where relationship equity is built and accrued. As a supplier, if you are dependable, timely and helpful, you enhance your reputation. When your name comes up for a promotion, your fellow employees are your best references. As a customer, if you are considerate, clear and appreciative of your supplier, people can see themselves working for you as their boss. Great internal references could be the tie-breaker between candidates who appear to be equally qualified in a technical sense.

Think about the people without powerful connections or exceptional talents who are moving up the career ladder in your organization. Most likely, what they have in common is that they work extremely well in the white spaces. Therefore, start today to cultivate such internal references through your willingness to help others look good. If you are an internal customer, first tell your fellow employee and then anybody in the organization who will listen how satisfied you are with your internal supplier. And if you are the internal supplier, let the internal customers know how working with them is an enjoyable and effective use of your time. And remember, at some point in the day you will be either the customer or the supplier—or both. This relationship equity is organizational currency and generates interest on the principal. The more relationship equity you have accumulated, the more effective you will be in getting what you want when you want it.

The things you do for yourself are gone, when you are gone—but, the things you do for others remain your legacy.

—Kalu Kalu

You think you know what you know—
but I guarantee you that you don't know
what you don't know. So find someone
who knows what you don't know.
                                    --Kwame S. Salter

SCALE PRES, 0 10 :

- WORK CLOSELY W/ LEADERSHIP
- HIT 85% MIN OF GOAL
  - % TO WORK SMART 95% - 120%

- BUILD A SYSTEM THAT WORKS

7

CHAPTER

BUILD AND NURTURE A SUPPORT NETWORK

Having a mentor is the key to moving up the corporate ladder. There is a need for multiple mentors—some of whom will guide you, others who will advocate for you and still others who will protect you.

Mentors are coaches, griots, advocates, teachers and Sherpa guides needed to successfully scale the corporate peaks. Most companies are aware of the importance of mentors to the development of talent within the organization. In fact, many organizations have formal mentor programs where young talent is assigned a seasoned mentor. These formal programs usually fail because too often they are like arranged marriages. The most effective mentor-protégé arrangement occurs naturally—almost organically. Still, a formal program recognizes the importance to organizational continuity and survival of a process for knowledge transfer. Some organizations refer to the person receiving the mentoring as a mentee, and others label them a protégé. Regardless of the label, the powerful impact of a mentor on a person's career is undeniable. Usually it is assumed that if one finds the right mentor, no other mentors are necessary. However, that colossal miscalculation misunderstands the role of a mentor. In my experience, mentors offer technical skills, or organizational savvy, or avenues to power.

Your advocate may not necessarily be your mentor. Advocates may speak up for you when you're not in the room, yet never speak to you outside of the room. Powerful people sometimes are not good teachers. To use a basketball analogy, some advocates are willing to "set a pick" for you—as long as you keep hitting the shot. Their reputation is based on picking winners—"shot makers." If you go into a "shooting slump," many advocates go into silent mode; when your name comes up, that sudden silence is quite loud. On the other hand, mentors stick with you, maintain contact with you through your ups and downs, learn from you, teach you and, when appropriate, advocate for you.

Usually mentors are seasoned or highly successful employees within the organization. The astute mentor first recognizes that the organization is dynamic and much has changed. Thus, he/she probes you for how you see the organization today. He/she recognizes that the strategies used in his or her ascendency to a key position are no longer effective or relevant. What is always relevant, however, is the mentor's insight. Not all mentors need to be physically at your location in the organization. Various communication media, including the telephone, email, Skype and text messaging can be effective mentoring tools.

Your first lesson is not to preclude a potential mentor from your network because you are of different genders or races or because the mentor has not reached the levels in the organization to which you aspire or because he/she is not in your particular business function. Good mentors have powerful conversations that might ding your ego a bit, but they will tell you what others consider "undiscussable" aspects of your behavior, style or performance. As Paula Sneed, retired Executive Vice President for Global Marketing Services at Kraft, once said, "You don't want just one mentor; rather you want to create a mosaic of mentors."

A learning experience is one of those things that says, "You know that thing you just did? Don't do that."
--Douglas Adams.

BY DEPT; WHO -
SALES - TED [GUIDE]
PM - ?
ENG - DARITH [ADVOCATE]

CHAPTER SUMMARIES

Before we get into the appendices, let's review for a minute. As the fiery old black preacher once said to his congregation before a very powerful sermon, "First, um huh, I'm gonna to tell you what I'm going to talk about, then I'm gonna to talk about it, and in conclusion, I'm gonna to tell you what I just talked about."

So let me tell you what I just talked about.

Chapter 1, Do Your Homework, dealt with preparation and intelligence gathering even before you approach the targeted company. The Internet has democratized access to information, and you should use it to research the target company in all possible ways. Find out what they make or do, how long they have been making it or doing it, who their customers are and how much money they make. Look at their financial condition. Has it improved, fluctuated, or declined? Have their products or services grown or shrunk—or morphed to meet new customers?

Chapter 2, Avoid Stereotyped Behaviors, critiqued the need to show white people you are really different from them—that you are "down" with black culture. First, I point out that your hue too often determines the views that non-blacks hold of you. Many whites think your color makes it unnecessary for them to view you as a unique individual. The range of variability for you is limited in their minds based on the steady diet of stereotypes that the media feeds them about the types of blacks they will encounter. The lesson in this chapter is to open up to who you really are—both socially and culturally.

Chapter 3, Integrate the Lunches and Links, spoke to the need to avoid isolating yourself from the mainstream's so-called "non-work" activities. Any gathering of employees—on or off the clock—is an opportunity to learn something that could be advantageous to your job and career. Go to a bar after work and listen to some country western, hard rock or pop that you might not have on your iPod.

Chapter 4, Master the Job, noted that competency is the most fundamental of what will insure career success. In this chapter, we discuss knowing the difference between the types of competencies—technical and behavioral. Knowing what to do and being proficient in the nuts and bolts of a job (technical competence) is one thing; how you do your job in relationship to other employees and your boss (behavioral competence) is quite another thing. Too many blacks approach these two competencies as though they are independent variables, but they always work hand in hand. Being an efficient and task-competent jerk is not protection against a job action being taken against you.

Chapter 5, Manage Perception, illustrated how we can influence the way people view our actions, attitudes and ambitions. Often what we intend to communicate about ourselves and our motives is obscured and misinterpreted because we let others draw conclusions without any input from us. We should always be vigilant about how we are being perceived. In fact, sometimes it is best simply to ask, "How am I doing? What advice can you give me?" This line of questioning allows us to clarify and manage what we intended the person to see and know about us.

Chapter 6, Be a Dependable Supplier, looked at the internal work environment as being made up of both suppliers and customers. At some point in the day, week, or month, you will be both. Work gets done in the organizational white spaces between jobs. When you need something from a fellow employee to get your job done, you're a customer. When you need to get something to a fellow employee to facilitate their completing a task, you're a supplier. It is easier being a customer than a supplier, yet being a dependable supplier allows you to build valuable relationship equity.

Chapter 7, Build and Nurture a Support Network, discussed the importance of a mentor. From Greek mythology, Mentor's relationship with Telemachus gave us the concept of someone who imparts wisdom to and shares knowledge with a less experienced colleague. Having a mentor in your corner is pre-requisite to moving up the corporate ladder. This chapter discussed the need for multiple mentors—some of whom will guide you, others who will advocate for you and still others who will protect you.

CLOSING MEMORANDUM

To: The Reader
From: Kwame S. Salter, Author
Subject: Action Plan

Keep an open mind:
"If you're not careful, you might learn something."

—Bill Cosby

Accept the possibility of a higher power:
"To believe in God is to love the world so much that it can't give you up."

—Robert Lily

Know where you are in time and space:
"The greatest challenge in life is to know which bridge to burn and which to cross."

—Anonymous

Develop and nurture a set of core values:
"The ultimate measure of a man is not where he stands in moments of comfort and convenience—but where he stands at times of challenge and controversy."

—Dr. Martin Luther King, Jr.

Challenge orthodoxy:
"Who is more foolish? Is it the child afraid of the dark-or the man afraid of the light?"   —Maurice Freehill

Seek balance in life:
"Whatever liberates our spirit without giving us self-control is disastrous."   —Johann Wolfgang von Goethe

Connect, contribute, and collaborate:
"All men are caught up in an inescapable network of mutuality."

—Dr. Martin Luther King, Jr.

Always seek to add value:
"The standing expectation for each member of a group should be to "Give, Get or Go!"

—K. S. Salter

Cultivate imagination and use humor lavishly:
"Imagination was given to man . . . ."

—Sir Francis Bacon

Secret to success:
"I don't know the secret to success, but I know the secret to failure—try and please everyone"

—Bill Cosby

EPILOGUE

"It's not what they call you—it's what you answer to..."

Preparing for success in any undertaking requires toughening up mentally. Corporate America is no exception. For blacks entering the corporate arena, mental toughness is a pre-requisite. The incumbents in the corner offices swiveling in their high-backed leather chairs are too sophisticated to stoop to the level of physical segregation and intimidation. However, they are often clueless or complicit in allowing for an environment that insures that "the diversity employee" knows his/her place. Yesterday, your place was a physically defined space. Today, knowing your place comes from picking up subtle social and cultural cues. Staying in your place depends on both your comfort level and competence.

Supposedly objective terms and labels are bandied about when assessing talent. Rarely is the golden moniker of "strategic" given to a black person. Too often, performance strengths are clustered around getting along, working hard, and being loyal to the company. I recall Amiri Baraka/LeRoi Jones once saying, "If you accept another man's definition, you are bound to reach his conclusion." Sadly, the conclusion too often reached is that you have a job, not that you aspire to a career.

The first name a person of color is likely to be called behind his/her back and sometimes to his/her face is an "affirmative action" or "diversity" hire. In fact, many of our people will state out loud, "They hired me because they needed a person of color—they were getting pressure from the government." This mentality is the beginning of the process of finding your place. In fact, only a cynical or disturbed person would hire an incompetent to prove a point about preferential hiring.

Even sadder is the fact that too many blacks answer to the "affirmative action hire" label. Too many blacks have ranked AA as the primary reason for their advancement—and not their competence. In reality, affirmative action has served whites more effectively than blacks. Affirmative action has given whites a built in excuse for not landing a job, promotion, or plum assignment. They never have to come to grips with having lost out to a person of color. There is, in their minds, no way to compete with an affirmative action hire. Yet in reality affirmative action preceded blacks in corporate America.

Admittedly, an effective affirmative action program can create and guarantee equal opportunity. However, only talent and determination can guarantee results. In fact, a grievance a person of color raises is often dismissed as "playing the race card." Well, there are 52 cards in the deck, and sometimes the race card is legitimate. Furthermore, note that white women have no hesitation about playing the gender card. Gay persons play the LGBT card most often as a preemptive move. For the record, white males have the entire deck at their disposal—and they are experts at dealing the cards.

White males, for decades with the weight of the law behind them, enjoyed preferential hiring (and they still enjoy the residuals from legal apartheid) over all non-white citizens.

They didn't even have to compete with these marginalized second class citizens—blacks were not permitted even to apply for certain jobs. Similarly, white women were restricted, in the main, to household duties and administrative tasks. Yet while victims of job discrimination, white women still enjoyed the financial benefits of legal apartheid in America. And today, the ultimate irony is that white women are major beneficiaries of affirmative action's positive intent to reverse race bias—while a disproportionate number of the negatives associated with the initiative are still ascribed to blacks. To their credit, white women do not appear at all reluctant to raise the issue of gender discrimination based on the absence of females in key and non-traditional positions.

Affirmative action has benefitted whites more than blacks—financially and psychologically. For example, the overly ambitious and solicitous young man who married the boss's daughter was often the beneficiary of affirmative action placements and promotions. Many white managers and leaders who might be chary of hiring or promoting a person of color on the basis of "there are not enough of them in key positions" would not hesitate to lead the way in expostulating for a better "gender mix." For some it is a matter of familiarity. They live with and know white women as their mothers, wives, daughters and nieces. For others it is a simple but compelling economic reality—in their own homes, two incomes are better than one.

Unfortunately, for too many whites, their only association with and knowledge of blacks is still by way of the crime or sports section of the newspaper. Watching the frenetic resident of a crime-ridden ghetto explaining in the finest Ebonics on the evening news how his neighbor was shot is not a good way to observe an entire race. Similarly, watching a gifted athlete struggle on camera to explain his skillful play on the field or court can be a wrenching experience. Yet these are the insidious and too-often comic images many whites are fed and unconsciously harbor. Ironically, any "exceptional Negro" is viewed as just that—an exception. His gifts and aptitude are not generalized to the larger black community as easily as are the traits and behaviors of a black from the "underclass."

Upon entering corporate America, more than a few blacks accept the role of being the expert on all things black. Their opinions are eagerly sought whenever an event or matter has a racial element. Nevertheless, they move as far away from the 'hood as fast as their new money will take them. However, in the work environment, they display behaviors and speech patterns considered to be representative of the black "culture." While on one hand they are repulsed by the black underclass, on the other hand these Negroes mimic so-called urban black culture in front of whites because they understand that the images of the black underclass are most familiar to their colleagues. In a sense, these aspiring young (and old) middle class African-Americans reinforce images every day that are both stereotypical and demeaning to the race.

In closing, I hope this book provided you with another perspective, if not some insights. I believe that the fight as black Americans must be centered on getting a fair shake and not necessarily a fair share. I believe this because when allowed to compete on a level playing field, our representation should not be limited to our percentage in the population. For example, 78% of the players in the multi-billion dollar global enterprise known as the NBA are black. When the criteria for advancement are reduced to objective competence without negative bias, we flourish. Opting for a fair shake over a fair share does not mean that the absence of blacks in corporate America is justifiable. It simply means we didn't get a fair shake.

I will end this book with the Salter Family motto:

"Persist Beyond Limits!"

APPENDIX

EXERCISE 1

WHO AM I?

Please rate your answer using the following guidelines. Rate yourself with #1 if the statement is closely descriptive of you in most situations; #2, if the statement is somewhat descriptive of you in most situations; and #3, if the statement is never descriptive of you in any situation. When finished, add up your total scores.

1. I use a different voice tone with whites I work with than with other whites whom I don't work with or know.

2. I can always look at a person and determine if he/she is prejudiced.

3. My punctuality depends on how important to my career the meeting or the person is I'm meeting with is.

4. I judge a person's intelligence primarily by his/her verbal skills.

5. I can be embarrassed by another black person's behavior at work.

6. I never or rarely socialize with my white work colleagues in my free time or on weekends.

7. I am reluctant to ask a white colleague for work advice to improve my job performance.

8. I defend questionable or criminal behavior by blacks if there are whites guilty of the same behaviors.

9. I am uncomfortable being the only black in an all-white business or social setting.

10. I do not trust whites ever to be completely honest with me.

If your score is 10-20 points, you're wasting a lot of time worrying about the wrong things. If your score is 25-30, you are freeing your mind from a lot of unnecessary baggage.

EXERCISE 2

SELF ASSESSMENT

Knowing who you are and knowing your strengths and weaknesses will help you manage your career. Please complete the SWOT analysis below. SWOT stands for Strengths, Weaknesses, Opportunities and Threats. Use bullet points or short descriptive statements, not long rambling sentences.

SWOT Analysis

Strengths	Weaknesses
Opportunities	Threats

STRENGTH

- PROFFESSIONAL
- DRIVE
- WILLINGNESS to LEARN
- SWC

OPPORTUNITEES

- OPEN TERRITORY
- QUALITY STRATEGIC ACCOUNTS

WEAKNESS

- TIME MANAGEMENT
- IT PRODUCT GAP
- TRUST LEVEL

THREATS

- COMPETITOR LANDSCAPE
- PRESIDIO NEW TO PUBLIC SECTOR SPACE

FUTURE PLAN QUESTIONS

Failure to plan is planning to fail.

Buy a personal diary or notebook with blank sheets and write down the responses to the questions below. Every quarter (3 months), check your responses to see if you are still on track.

1. Describe how you will use your unique point(s) of difference—i.e., knowledge, skills, abilities—that you believe set you apart from your peers

2. List the mentors in your life by name and write down what each taught you and the last time you reached out to them.

3. Identify the professional and technical magazines, blogs and periodicals that you subscribe to and read.

4. Describe where you want your career to be in 3-5 years, including job title, duties and salary—in that order.

5. Write down on a 3x5 card the one audacious, outlandish and outrageous personal or professional goal that you have never shared with anyone

6. Set a date in your mind for accomplishing that outrageous goal and write it on the 3x5 card.

7. Daily, affirm the goal and work your ass off. Conceive it. Believe it....Achieve it!

BONUS MATERIAL

BONUS MATERIAL

The Power of the Pen

One of the most neglected forms of communication today is the handwritten note. Sending a prompt handwritten note is a very effective way to reinforce a number of positive qualities you possess, stand out from others, and to personalize an otherwise strictly professional encounter.

In today's text and email driven world, voice communication is challenging. A voice mail may or may not be listened to by the receiver. Even more difficult is cutting through the organizational and administrative insulation most executives wrap themselves in to avoid unwanted contact. In order of impact, the following represents my hierarchy of communication modes:

1. Face to Face (good luck!)

2. Written notes (personal and impactful)

3. Emails (easily flushed)

4. Text messages (overused and too social)

5. Telephone conversations (damn near impossible)

Given the slim-to-none chances of getting a second face to

face meeting after your initial interview or meeting , you must find a way to differentiate yourself from the pack. <u>Sending a thank you note after an initial interview improves both the probability of being remembered and the chances of being screened in for a second interview.</u> Similarly, if your mentor's schedule is hectic and full, don't expect to just drop by after your meeting to say "Thanks."

Busy executives know that this impromptu encounter could result in an unplanned and unwanted second meeting. So, the next best thing to do is just drop them a note. <u>Have some note cards made at your local office supply store with your name or initials imprinted.</u>

Below are some examples of thank you messages, using a handwritten note, email or, when appropriate, text messaging.

From protégé to mentor

A handwritten note:

> ## <kSs>
>
> Bob, just a note to let you know how much I appreciated the time, insights and guidance you shared with me today. I am looking forward to our next scheduled meeting. Thanks.
>
> Kwame

Some caveats on handwritten notes:

- ✓ Avoid elaborate art work. Keep it simple and plain.

- ✓ Do not get fancy with handwriting. Deciphering a word or sentence is frustrating for the reader.

- ✓ Stay away from drugstore cards. Select tasteful and sturdy paper stock. Go to www.cranes.com/business and check out options.

- ✓ Never send the first draft of your note. Check for grammatical and spelling errors.

An email to a mentor:

```
╔══════════════════════════════════════════╗
                    Email

 To: Mentor

 From: Kwame S. Salter

 Subject: Advice and Counsel

 Bob, thanks again for the time you spent with me today. I
 deeply appreciate the candid feedback and useful advice
 you give me each time we meet. I am looking forward to
 our next scheduled meeting.
╚══════════════════════════════════════════╝
```

A text message to a mentor:

New Message

_____

Subject: Meeting Today
_____

Bob, thanks for the time and advice you gave me
today. Looking forward to our next scheduled
meeting.

Send

The key to these messages being effective is promptness. If you wait for more than 24 hours, your message loses a lot of its impact. Again, I strongly recommend the handwritten note, sent by internal mail or the USPS (if your mentor is in another region). Handwritten notes stand a better chance of eluding capture by the administrative assistant who, most likely, has access to the executive's email. Text messaging assumes a personal relationship that gives you the executive's mobile phone number.

WORKSHEETS

MY VISION:

_____

_____

_____

_____

_____

_____

_____

_____

_____

_____

_____

_____

_____

_____

_____

_____

_____

MY LONG TERM GOALS

(3-5 YEARS)

1._____

_____

_____

_____

_____

2._____

_____

_____

_____

_____

3._____

_____

_____

_____

MY SHORT TERM GOALS

<u>(1-2 YEARS)</u>

1._____

_____

_____

_____

_____

2._____

_____

_____

_____

_____

3._____

_____

_____

_____

MY MENTORS

Name: Title:

1.

2.

3.

4.

5.

6.

7.

N O T E S

N O T E S

NOTES

ABOUT THE AUTHOR

Kwame S. Salter was born in Delhi, Louisiana, and grew up in Milwaukee, Wisconsin. He earned the Bachelor of Arts degree from the University of Wisconsin-Whitewater, graduating magna cum laude, and Master of Arts in Educational Administration from the University of Wisconsin-Madison. In 1983, the University of Wisconsin-Whitewater recognized Kwame as an Outstanding Recent Alumnus. Kwame served as the Director of the UW-Madison's Afro-American Race Relations and Cultural Center from 1970-1973. From 1976 until 1986, he served as the Executive Director of Dane Co. Parent Council, Inc., the grantee for Project Head Start in Dane County, and as interim Executive Director of the Community Action Commission, Inc. of Dane County.

Throughout his adult life, Kwame has been a tireless campus activist, community organizer, political leader and elected official, giving voice to the disenfranchised and serving as a persistent force for strategic inclusion of historically underrepresented talent in corporate America. Kwame won election to the Madison Metropolitan Board of Education, becoming one of the youngest persons elected to that body, serving 2 years as Vice-President and 4 consecutive years as President. Additionally, Kwame served two terms on the Board of Advisors of the University of Wisconsin-Madison's Graduate School of Business. Kwame has been cited and honored by a number of organizations and media. He was selected as one of the Milwaukee Journal's "80 for the 80's" which highlighted young leaders in Wisconsin. In 2006, Kwame was featured in Who's Who in Black Chicago: Celebrating African-American Achievements—The Inaugural Edition.

In 1986, Kwame was recruited to the Oscar Mayer Foods Corporation by the Chairman and CEO. He moved rapidly from Corporate Affirmative Action Manager to Human Resources Director of the Oscar Mayer Business Unit in Madison, Wisconsin. Kwame's professional human resources experience has been varied and deep. In 1995, he was appointed Sr. Director, HR for the Kraft General Foods' North American Foodservice Division and moved to Glenview, Illinois.

During his company's evolution from Kraft General Foods to Kraft Global, Kwame was appointed to positions of increasing responsibility within the company's HR function—from VP, HR for Sales & Customer Service to VP Global Functions, Staffing and Diversity. In 2008, Kwame retired as the Senior Vice-President, HR, Kraft Global Supply Chain. Currently, Kwame is an adjunct professor at Concordia University Chicago and President of The Salter Consulting Group, LLC.

During his company's evolution from Kraft General Foods to Kraft Global, Kwame was appointed to positions of increasing responsibility within the company's HR function—from VP, HR Sales & Customer Service, VP Global Functions, Staffing and Diversity. In 2008, Kwame retired as the Senior Vice-President, HR, Kraft Global Supply Chain. Presently, Kwame is an adjunct professor at Concordia University Chicago and President of The Salter Consulting Group, LLC.

Kwame lives in Oak Park, Illinois with his wife Phyllis Harris. He is the father of four children, Kevin Jamal, Keri-Jamelda Shahidi, Matthew and Lauren, and he has five dynamic grandchildren.